80 Years of ERF

Editor: Mike Forbes
Designer: Debbie Walker
Publisher: Paul Appleton
Managing Director: Adrian Cox
Commercial Director: Ann Saundry
Marketing Manager: Kirsty Flatt

First Published June 2013

ISBN: 0-946219-43-5

Published by Key Publishing Ltd.
PO Box 100, Stamford,
Lincolnshire PE9 1XP

Printed in England by
Precision Colour Printing Ltd, Telford.

Visit the Key Publishing website at
www.keypublishing.com

From the publishers of

Above: The first ERF, chassis no 63, MJ 2711, has been preserved for many years and regularly appears at rallies, as seen here. *(Len Jefferies)*

Front Cover: Typical of the many ERF eight-wheelers to join the Hansons fleet over the years, this B Series bulk powder tanker, SKU 143S, is seen in the yard at Chapel-en-le-Frith, Derbyshire, in company with other members of the fleet, including another B Series eight-wheeler, tipper AAK 73T. *(PM Photography)*

Back Cover: A real 'blast from the past' – a scene unlikely to be recreated today, as a KV-cabbed ERF 44G, BEN 990, of Bury, Lancashire-based waste merchants Henry Beetson Ltd, is loaded with bales of scrap cardboard with a hoist from a run-down looking warehouse in a back street. *(CHC aay579)*

ERF Looking Back

This year marks 80 years since the first ERF was built. This book is not intended to be a definitive history of the company but, hopefully, offers a flavour of the different types of vehicle the company has produced over the years since 1933. The majority of the pictures have not been seen before, at least, not for a very long time. They mainly come from two archives, which we are able to use for *Vintage Roadscene*, offering the magazine an identity all of its own.

We all know the story, how Edwin Richard Foden had retired from the Foden family company in 1932, but was persuaded by his son Dennis and others to build the diesel-powered lorries in which he had failed to interest his fellow board-members at Foden. The company, E R Foden & Son, famously resulted from a meeting with a number of ex-Foden men in the conservatory of his daughter's house.

The first vehicle, chassis no 63 after E R Foden's age, and to make it appear one of many, was built in a spare workshop of local coach-builder, J H Jennings of Sandbach, which was to build most of the ERF cabs and ended up becoming part of the company from the 1960s. Proprietary components, including a Gardner engine, David Brown gearbox, Kirkstall axles and Clayton-Dewandre brakes, were used on the early vehicles, setting the scene for many years to come.

The CI.4 (Compression Ignition, Four cylinder) and its larger engined and multi-axle derivatives continued to be produced into the post-war years, including a some 6 ton 4x2 military lorries during World War 2, with the original 'Saloon'-style cab soon being replaced by a more streamlined version.

In 1948, the exposed radiator gave way to a curved grille on the 'V' cab on a new range, using the number of cylinders in the Gardner engine and the number of wheels as the type number, for example, '68G' for a 6LW-powered eight-wheeler. The V cab was coachbuilt, with metal panels on a wooden frame, but there was an all-steel alternative from Willenhall, also used by BMC, with distinctively-shaped wings from 1951.

A bigger development, in terms of looks at least, was the launch in 1953 of the KV, or 'Kleer Vue' cab, designed by Gerald Broadbent, then at Jennings, but later Bowyer Bros and Boalloy. This was much more rounded and modern-looking, with wrap-around windscreens, plus a recently-introduced oval grille. Glass-fibre panels followed, along with a semi-bonneted three-man version, nicknamed 'Sabrina' after the voluptuous starlet of the day, aimed at the brewery trade, although not widely used by them.

A distinctive feature of ERFs for many years was the tapered side-frames of the so-called 'Greyhound' chassis, designed by Ernest Sherratt, chief designer for many years from the start at ERF. This saved weight, but added strength where it was most required.

The KV cab was replaced on most up-dated ERF models from 1962 by the LV, with its glass-fibre-panelled cab with a one-piece windscreen. Initially, there were two versions of this, from Jennings and Boalloy, with a number of detail differences. This cab was again up-dated in the early 1970s for the new A Series, as well as being fitted to the on-going models in the rest of the range.

Alternative engines from Cummins and Rolls-Royce were available alongside the legendary Gardners, while there was also a choice of gearbox, axles and other components on most models.

As an alternative to the glass-fibre cabs, the Motor Panels-based MW cab was also available on ERF tractor units, notably on heavy haulage and export chassis, and also popular with international operators, who wanted a sleeper cab, not available on the A Series, although sleeper pods were added by some users.

The main features of the A Series were incorporated in the B Series from 1974, which most noticeably had a new cab, the SP (Steel Plastic), designed by Ken Skelton. The B Series was most successful for ERF, with the SP cab, in day or sleeper cab versions, being up-dated on the follow-on C Series from 1981, the E Series from 1986, the EC and ECX, right up to the MAN take-over, by which time Cummins power was standard on nearly all models.

Meanwhile, ERF had produced some fire appliances through the 1970s, and a medium-weight 16 tonner, the M Series. This was offered initially with a Gardner or Dorman V8 diesel, but was more successful in the 1980s, when a Perkins-engined option became available. There were various deals with other manufacturers, to market lighter vehicles, still-born in the case of Hino, short-lived with the Turkish BMC and Isuzu, but more successful with Steyr, which probably brought ERF to the attention of MAN.

E R and Dennis Foden had been joint managing directors until E R died in 1950, with Dennis carrying on along after his father's death until he, in turn died at the early age of 60 in 1960, to be succeeded by his younger half-brother, Peter, who held the reins until he retired as Chairman and Chief Executive, when the company was sold to Western Star of Canada in 1996, passing away in 2012. Meanwhile, ERF was sold to MAN, which slowly but surely 'restructured' the British operations, production ending in 2002, German-built Cummins and then MAN-engined vehicles being badged as ERFs until the end in 2008.

Today, 80 years on from the start of production, ERF lorries remain popular with many transport enthusiasts, for many of whom the various cabs and other obvious variations will be more significant than the mechanical specifications, so that is what we have concentrated on to a large extent in the captions to the pictures used in this book. ERFs make up a significant proportion of the vehicles to be seen at many rallies these days, especially where REVS, the ERF Historic Vehicles Society is in attendance. Some of the photographs in this book are of preserved lorries, but most were taken of vehicles in service, doing what ERFs were known for, working hard.

Mike Forbes is a life-long transport enthusiast and, having spent most of his working years in the road transport industry, is now editor of *Vintage Roadscene* magazine. The pictures in this book come from the two main archives used for this publication, PM Photography and the Stilltime Collection from Chris Hodge Commercials.

Managing Director of the company for many years,
Peter Foden, handed over the 50,000th ERF to the
Mobil Oil company in 1984. Chassis no 50,063,
seen alongside the first ERF, chassis no 63, was
a 32C2, plated at 32 tonnes, with the SP3 cab,
Cummins L10 250 turbo engine, Spicer 10 speed
gearbox and Rockwell axle, built shortly before the
CP range was launched (ERF/Ian Allan Library)

Looking very similar to the very first ERF, and restored in the livery of F & P Lythgoe of Warburton, obviously inspired by no 63, but fitted with a Gardner 6LW diesel so designated CI.6, chassis no 735, with Lancashire registration CTB 879, was on display at the 2012 Kelsall rally. (Author)

This CI.4 tipper, CYC 387, also seen at Kelsall, was originally in the Somerset quarry fleet of W J King, but has been restored in the livery of J Wareing & Son, of Wrea Green, near Preston. (Author)

Seen on the 'REVS' stand at the 2011 Commercial Vehicle Show at the NEC, this CI5 four-wheeler is now in the preserved fleet of J Leech of Haslington, near Crewe. This has the original so-called 'Saloon' cab. (Author)

The original eight-wheeler was designated the CI.682. This example, FLG 212, seen in the dark days of World War 2, with a headlamp cowl and white edging to the wings, with a draw-bar trailer attached, was then in the haulage fleet of Thomas Tilling Ltd. (CHC aaw758)

80 years of ERF

From 1938 to 1948, the so-called 'Streamline' cab, with a curved front profile was fitted to the CI range, rather than the original 'Saloon' cab. Almost looking like before and after pictures of the same vehicle, here we have a begrimed DUS 248, also carrying trade-plate 937 M, in the wartime fleet of the Clyde Soyameal Factory of Govan, and a similar artic tanker, looking like a brand new delivery to Wakefield 'Castrol' Oils. (Both PM Photography)

Most likely the lighter OE4 model with the Gardner 4LK engine, this ERF was fitted with a more streamlined cab, including a curved radiator grille. Still part of the delivery fleet of Ushers Brewery, in Trowbridge, Wiltshire, in the 1950s, it is seen being prepared for service alongside later V-cabbed models, during a visit by Commercial Motor. (CHC aah795)

This dropside, GNT 176, was another CI model, used by Sankey of Wellington to delivery its steel pressings to automotive industry customers. (CHC abe883)

This pre-war CI.5, DUS 640, was still in use with a draw-bar trailer in the fleet of Highland Haulage, of Inverness, during the 1950s. (CHC aae601)

Another CI.5, AFK 924, looking a little down-at-heel, in the fleet of Grey Motors of Bethesda, in North Wales, delivers bagged animal feed. (CHC aar 443)

Johnson Brothers of Hanley, Stoke-on-Trent, was running this CI artic, PVT 811, equipped with Scammell automatic semi-trailer coupling, to deliver its 'Trent Ware' during the 1950s. (CHC abb176)

A fine-looking eight-wheeler, restored in the livery of S Jones & Sons of Bethania, Cardiganshire, is this CI.682, with Wiltshire registration, DMW 939, which was seen at Kelsall in 2012. (Author)

Along with the Jones eight-wheeler, this CI.5, EWW107, in the livery of J Scott & Sons of Bradford, was seen at Kelsall in 2012, but they both also appear at many other rallies. (Author)

Another fine restoration is this CI 'Chinese Six', MBB 222, was registered in the North-east, but is now restored in the livery of J T Evans of Chirk. It was seen at Llandudno in 2011, in the company of restored later model ERFs. (Author)

Above: In 1948, ERF introduced the new 'V' cab, with a similar profile to the previous streamlined cab. It was still a classic coach-built cab on a wooden frame. This 66G was fitted with a Butterfields tank for chemicals company, Geigy of Manchester. (PM Photography)

Main picture: A tanker for a different commodity, Ind Coope's 'Double Diamond' beer, on a classic V cabbed 68G eight-wheeled chassis, FA 9651, seen on a deserted dual-carriageway. (CHC aat981)

This 54G four-wheeled dropside, NVT 558, is fitted with the V cab and has been preserved in the livery of G Wooliscroft & Son, of Stoke-on-Trent, and was seen at Kelsall in 2012. (Author)

This short wheelbase 54G tipper, HUT 260, in the livery of E Easingwood, of Blaby, Leicester, was displayed at an early 1950s Commercial Motor Show. The distinctively-shaped front wings show that this lorry was fitted with the all-steel Willenhall cab, also seen on BMC, Guy and Dennis vehicles. (CHC aab296)

Also fitted with the Willenhall cab was this 54G dropside, MDD 904, of H B Everton Roadways Ltd, Droitwich, seen leaving the Kidderminster factory of the British Sugar Corporation.
(CHC aaz773)

This 66G with V cab is seen on test from the factory on trade plates 662 MA by Commercial Motor in the early 1950s. The platform body is loaded to the vehicle's maximum gross weight, with concrete blocks, while the lack of rear mudguards is unusual. It's hill-climbing abilities are interesting the locals, while the driver of an earlier ERF of Cadnam's Transport is kindly giving it a clear run at the hill. (CHC aba797/8)

80 years of ERF

ERFs were not all that common in the British Road Services fleet, but this Willenhall-cabbed example, Lincolnshire-registered KFW 714, was loaded with a ladle-carrier at the Distington Engineering works, near Workington, Cumberland, rather than from its home depot at Scunthorpe. (PM Photography)

Above: Another vehicle on test, this time the four-wheeled dropside, JUK 376, from the Meadows fleet is fitted with this manufacturer's engine under its V cab. (CHC abe293)

Left: A few ERFs were fitted with this style of cab, with the oval grille on the V cab structure. However, TYO 571, being in the Union Cartage fleet, well-known for rebuilding its vehicles, might not have started life with this cab. (PM Photography)

The KV – or 'Kleer-Vue' cab, designed by Gerald Broadbent, later of Boalloy and 'Tautliner' fame, while he was still at Jennings, ERF's associated bodybuilder. It was a great step forward in cab styling, although early versions were still coach-built with alloy panels on a wooden frame. There were a number of variations to the KV cab over the years, as we will see. Here, 342 CTF, a 54G of F Southworth, based in Chorley, Lancashire, is loaded by hand with bales of cloth. (CHC aar624)

Right: Another good-looking 54G rigid four-wheeler was this Butterfields tanker, LJA 696, for The Ironsides Lubricants company of Stockport. (PM Photography)

Below: Showerings of Shepton Mallet, in Somerset, was well-known for is champagne perry 'Babycham', advertised on the tall headboard of its platform vehicles, like this attractive 54G, registered 975 BYC, seen at a late 1950s Commercial Motor Show. (CHC aaz338)

This is an example of the lightweight 44G model, powered by a four cylinder Gardner 4LK, with a variation of the cab known as the LKV. This vehicle, YSF 40, still in excellent condition, was still working for Thomas Montgomery & Sons, potato merchants, of Kilmarnock, through the 1970s. (PM Photography)

This 44G, registered BSF 38B, seen at Kelsall preserved in the livery of H & J Tuer, of Ivegill, Carlisle, is a late example of the lightweight ERF, believed to have originally run for brewers Scottish & Newcastle, which had quite a fleet of these vehicles. (Author)

Here are two 68G eight-wheeled tankers in the Ind Coope fleet, seen unloading at Burton-on-Trent, FFA 179 and GFA 846. They show the earlier and later style of oval grille. It seems surprising that it needed to be enlarged, given the Gardner engine's legendary cool running. (CHC aat 993)

A lovely example of an eight-wheeled dropside 68G, 332 DVT, with the KV cab, no 17 in the fleet of Alfred Hartshorn, of Wednesbury. (CHC aas171)

Another splendid ERF 68G from 1955, LED 874, used by Joseph Crosfield & Sons Ltd of Warrington, to collect raw materials and to deliver Persil washing powder, which the company produced and which would have had to be well-sheeted to keep it dry. (Ian Allan Library)

Right: This 66G with a later version of the KV cab has a Gardner 150 badge on its grille. It is seen when brand new at the Butterfields works, after the fitting of its oval tank for the Medina Refinery Co Ltd, of London SE8. (PM Photography)

Below: With an interesting assortment of new and used ERFs in the background, here is a 68G chassis cab awaiting its turn at the body-builder's works. (CHC aas278)

This 68G eight-wheeler was being used by Harris Road Services, of Lostock Gralam, Northwich, with a draw-bar trailer with a difference, being a Scammell automatic coupling semi-trailer, attached with a special 'dolly', to create the typical long distance haulage outfit up to the 1960s. The trailer is also seen behind a much earlier ERF, with the Streamline cab. (CHC abf 798/9)

Right: The 'Sabrina' cab was also used on a number of heavy haulage tractors, built for the Park Gate Iron & Steel Co Ltd, of Rotherham, and for export, like this one seen during the build-up of a show around 1960, in the livery of Thorntons of Welkon, in the Orange Free State, South Africa. (CHC aab301)

Below: The semi-normal control version of the KV cab, ostensibly designed for the brewery trade, with its three-man crews, although used on general haulage by a number of companies was, for obvious reasons, nicknamed 'Sabrina', after the stage-name of voluptuous glamour model and actress Norma Sykes. An early example is seen at a roundabout, loaded with test weights on trade plates 570 MB in the late 1950s. (CHC aas277)

80 years of ERF

Left: A version of the cab, known as the 2KV, featured squared-off and slightly-flared wheel arches, as seen on this tractor unit, registered 78 SMA, but carrying the 570 MB tradeplates, on test with a four-in-line trailer, loaded with concrete blocks. (PM Photography)

Below: Commercial Motor took lots of photographs at heats of the Lorry Driver of the Year competition. Here we see a 64G tractor unit, 51 HWL, of J Curtis & Sons Ltd, heavy haulage contractors of Oxford, with a typical Carrimore low-loader trailer of the period, with a 'knock-out' rear axle. Later KV cabs like this one were fitted with twin headlights. (CHC aan782)

The Bird's Eye name is still well-known. Back in the early 1960s, the company had a fleet of ERF eight-wheeled refrigerated vans, like LVG 273, seen at the 1960 Earl's Court show, which made bulk deliveries from the quick-freezing factories to distributors, with legends like 'Chicken Pie Special' on the side. (CHC aab300)

Another show scene, featuring an eight-wheeled chassis-cab in the livery of a company always well-known for its fleet of ERFs, A H Davey of Stoke-on-Trent, next to a four-wheeled platform vehicle for neighbour, Berresfords Transport, with an Ind Coope tanker in the background. (CHC abf625)

This 54G platform-bodied four-wheeler, with the later flared-arch and twin-headlight 2KV cab, 999 NVT, was preserved in the livery of Comber Transport for many years, but is now in the C S Ellis preserved fleet, as seen at Kelsall in 2012. (Author)

This 64G tractor unit, 681 HGB, in the fleet of Glasgow-based James Hemphill, Bulk Liquids Transport, was photographed when brand new in the early 1960s, along with its 'banana-shaped' tanker trailer. (PM Photography)

This early 1960s KV-cabbed tractor unit, RCN 197, of Cawthorn & Sinclair, based in Birtley, County Durham, was used on continental services, via the then new 'roll-on, roll-off' ferries, and is seen in a French side street, as the tarpaulin cover is spread over its 40ft tilt trailer. (CHC abh147)

Another version of the ERF eight-wheeler had a 'set back' front axle, with a different version of the cab, known as the 2KV12. This offered better load distribution onto the front axles, within the overall length, and seems to have been popular with tanker operators, like Isherwoods VIP Petroleum co Ltd, of Eccles, Lancashire, whose WDB 720 is seen delivering to one of the company's garages in the 1960s. (CHC aay686)

Also fitted with the 2KV12 cab was this tanker, registered 6089 EZ in Northern Ireland, part of the Shellmex-BP distribution fleet, seen taking part in a Lorry Driver of the Year round in Middlesex. (CHC abg983)

80 years of ERF

Seen at another LDOY round on the South Coast is this 'Chinese Six' with the set-back' style of cab, 249 DFJ, in the fleet of S A Setter of Exeter, which worked on contract to Westbrick. (CHC. abj475)

80 years of ERF

Many operators stuck with ERF for at least a proportion of their fleets for many years. A typical example was Ketton Cement, which had KV-cabbed 7790 W and the later LV-cabbed eight-wheeler, MWJ 714D, both fitted with bulk powder tanks. After Castle Cement had taken over the company, it continued to use ERFs, as we'll see later. (PM Photography and CHC aav640)

Although a few operators continued to specify variants of the KV cab up to 1966, the 1960s could be said to be the era of the LV cab, in its various forms. This is an early LV-cabbed 54G, 1982 LG, seen re-starting on a steep hill during a press test. This is the Boalloy version of the LV cab, which had a full-width lifting front panel and vertical door handles. (CHC aax813)

80 years of ERF

Above: The vertical door handles can just be seen on the LV cab of this 68G short wheelbase bulk tipper, 600 FFJ, for Frank Tucker of Exeter, seen at the 1962 Commercial Motor Show. (CHC aab299)

Right: This early LV cab was the Jennings version, which had a narrower hinged front inspection panel and horizontal door handles. It is on an eight-wheeled tanker for Proctor & Gamble, unusually fitted with 'super single' rear wheels and tyres, on the Butterfields stand at the 1964 Earls Court show. (CHC aak 010)

An interesting variation on the LV cab was this coachbuilt integral box van, for Bensons of Bury, seen at the 1962 show. A similar vehicle, based on the earlier KV cab is preserved and often seen on the rally circuit. (CHC aaa089)

Also at the 1962 show was this special heavy haulage tractor, which was called a 66X66CU, destined for service in the Libyan desert. Notice that there is another 'Babycham' vehicle on display in the background. (CHC aab298)

80 years of ERF

A classic view of an LV-cabbed artic, DRM 804C, of Johnston Bros, Gilcrux Ltd, of Aspatria, Cumberland, with a single axle trailer, being loaded from a warehouse with a mixture of boxes and sacks. (PM Photography)

This tractor unit, with the forward axle cab, known as the 2LV, was brand new to the fleet of A S Jones & Co, another well-known tanker operator, with an equally new chemical tanker trailer from Butterfields. (PM Photography)

Seen later in its life, somewhat battle-scarred BNF 887D was in the fleet of Lloyd's Transport & Warehousing of Manchester. (PM Photography)

Like the previous artic unit, this 1965 LV-cabbed vehicle does not have the set-back front axle. In the fleet of H & L Haulage of Workington, EFU 487C, is coupled to a 33ft trailer, loaded with a storage tank. (PM Photography)

80 years of ERF

Some ERF tractor units were fitted with the set-back axle LV cab, like Gardner 150-powered CBE 587C of Tanker Hire Ltd of Scunthorpe, seen with a bulk powder tanker trailer. (PM Photography)

Another tractor unit with the set-back axle was YDB 599 in Edward Beck of Stockport's heavy haulage fleet, seen with some large cable drums on its low-loader trailer. (PM Photography)

This Gardner 150-powered LV-cabbed unit, KEH 619D, of J L Cooper of Milton, Stoke-on-Trent, must have struggled with the two 20ft containers on a 40ft trailer seen in its later years. (PM Photography)

A fine example of a 68G eight-wheeler, NUN 401G, preserved in the livery of Cawley Brothers of Llanrwst, North Wales, seen at Llandudno in 2011. (Author)

A fine view of a Cummins-engined heavy duty six-wheeled tractor unit with crew cab, MDC 255G designed for heavy haulage applications, such as transporting an excavator for Pearsons of Teesside. (PM Photography)

Another Cummins-engined three-axle heavy haulage tractor, VTR 982J, in the fleet of Bakers of Southampton, showing what it can do with a flat trailer loaded with a barge. (PM Photography)

80 years of ERF

Wilsons' 54G four-wheeler, RNA 163J, powered by a Gardner 100 diesel, looks striking in the company's yellow livery. By this time the cab had developed to the 5LV version. (PM Photography)

Leicester-based Federated Road Transport Services had quite a mixed fleet, which included this ERF with the LV cab, WNR 952J. (PM Photography)

One way in which an articulated vehicle could be operated at 32 tons gross in the late 1960s was to use a tri-axle trailer of the design seen here, loaded with a tank container, behind Gardner 180-powered ERF, ONE 476H, of Industrial Latex compounds, based in Heywood, Lancashire.
(PM Photography)

This Cummin-engined tractor unit, EWU 785H, was used by W P Butterfield (Engineers) Ltd, of Shipley, Yorkshire, to deliver new tanker trailers built for its customers, like this one for Pickfords.
(PM Photography)

80 years of ERF

This ERF, OUO 37G, of W L Vallance, makes a striking sight, as its Hoynor tipping trailer discharges into a conveyor on the quayside, loading a bulk cargo ship. (CHC 3493)

This twin-steer, Cummins-powered ERF, with its extended LV cab, PKR 668G, in the fleet of Lowe, of Paddock Wood, Kent, is fondly remembered by many transport enthusiasts who saw it. (PM Photography)

Below: A comparison of the LV, earlier KV and later B-Series cab styles is offered by these three preserved vehicles at the ERF get-together at the 2012 Kelsall rally. *(Author)*

80 years of ERF

Another A Series tractor unit, GLV 785N, in the fleet of Eric Wilkinson of Leyland, Lancashire, with a curtain-sided trailer. The cab, known as the 7LV, has had a 'sleeper pod' added. (PM Photography)

Yorkley Timber of Ross-on-Wye used a number of ERF tractor units over the years, which obviously had to work hard, like this Cummins-powered A Series, NCJ 289M, seen here with a pole trailer, loaded with a very large 'butt'. (PM Photography)

Not all operators switched to the new A Series, some preferring the existing 64G with the forward axle, like Humphreys of Watford. Its DUR 883K, with Gardner 180 engine, was fitted with the 8LV cab with the new style grille, however, and is seen with a nicely roped and sheeted load on a 40ft flat. (PM Photography)

The new grille was also fitted to the 68G eight-wheelers in the 1970s, but they continued with the old-style springing and other features. This is TWU 237L, a long wheelbase tipper, conforming to the outer axle spread required up to the early 1970s for 28 tons gross operation, of S & S Gillson of Haworth. (PM Photography)

This eight-wheeler of C M Krelle of Prescot, Lancashire, GEK 861N, seen surrounded by later B Series ERFs, also had the set-back axle cab and new grille, resembling more closely the A Series, but different under the skin. (PM Photography)

ERF continued to produce four-wheelers, for operators wanting a premium lorry. Many of these 16-tonners had long lives. Here Gardner 120-powered NWU 456M of A Featherstone, of Bishop Auckland, is another with a sleeper pod added to its cab. (PM Photography)

Eight-wheelers continued to be popular for bulk tanker work through the 1970s and beyond, exemplified by ATU 198M, in the fleet of British Salt Ltd, of Middlewich. (PM Photography)

G Plant of Nantwich was well-known for its fleet of older ERFs. Although seen at a rally, these eight-wheelers, AVR 802M and BNF 571N, were still working for Crewe Cold Food Store in the 1990s, although seen here at a rally. (PM Photography)

This six-wheeled 'bulk blower'-equipped tipper, PFF 705L, would have spent its life delivering animal feed, until preserved in the livery of A L Jones of Corwen, in which it appeared at Llandudno in 2011. (Author)

A complete draw-bar outfit is unusual in preservation, but this 'wagon and drag' with cattle boxes, in a livery similar to Plant's, was seen at the Basingstoke rally in 2011. (Author)

Left: One of many ERF eight-wheelers in the Chapel-en-le-Frith fleet of Hansons was this bulk coal tipper, KWB 662P. By the time this one entered service, the B Series would have been available. (PM Photography)

Below: An ERF tractor unit and taker trailer ready for delivery from Butterfields' works to Chevron in the early 1970s. (PM Photography)

80 years of ERF

An impressive eight-wheeled livestock transporter, SLG 504D, of Graham Simms of Northwich, which had obviously had a cab rebuild in the 1970s. (PM Photography)

ERFs could be long-lived, and this 1967 four-wheeler, DMB 863F, of E Park & Sons Ltd, potato merchants of Macclesfield, had been up-dated with a new grille in the 1970s. (PM Photography)

Another classic eight-wheeled powder tanker, HTO 88N of Ambergate, Derbyshire-based Dean Haulage. (PM Photography)

The 'Chinese Six' continues to have a place in some fleets even today, where avoidance of front axle overload with multiple drops could be a problem. Here is JFR 428N of A Featherstone, of Bishop Auckland. (PM Photography)

Meanwhile, some operators, especially export customers, who preferred an all-steel cab, could specify the MW cab, built by Motor Panels. Beresford of Stoke-on-Trent operated UVT 204L, with a step-frame maximum cube tilt trailer on TIR work to the continent. (PM Photography)

Turks Transport, of Benenden in Kent, was another operator who preferred the 5MW cab. Its KKL 592P is seen here with a Ferrymasters tilt trailer. (PM Photography)

The MW cab was also fitted to some heavy haulage tractors, like three-axle, Cummins-engined KUE 461L of Doyle of Coleshill, Birmingham, seen with a tracked excavator on its low-loader trailer. (PM Photography)

As time moved on, the MW cab gained a larger grille, like PDF 443R of Richard Read, the Forest of Dean operator, seen here with a bulk tipping trailer. (PM Photography)

The last MW cabs, known as the 7MW, featured a more striking front panel, like GEH 513N of John C Simmons of Rothley, Leicestershire. (PM Photography)

This 7MW-cabbed heavy haulage ballast box tractor, KCH 95N, has been preserved in the livery of M Corbishley & Sons, seen here at Kelsall with their eight-wheeled box van, YNC 214L. (Author)

This page: This picture offers the opportunity to compare the A Series and B Series, with these two seen together in the preserved fleet of W Nichol of Lochmaben at Kelsall. (Author)

Page opposite: The ERF B Series was launched in 1974, incorporating the best features of the A Series, but with a new cab, the SP, with 'Sheet Moulded Compound' panels on a steel frame replacing its glass-fibre predecessor. Tractor units started to appear in 1975 and these two are seen during the build-up of the Scottish Show. The sleeper cab model is in the livery of Harry Lawson of Broughty Ferry, while the day cab version is in Munro of Aberdeen's colours. (CHC aad214)

80 years of ERF

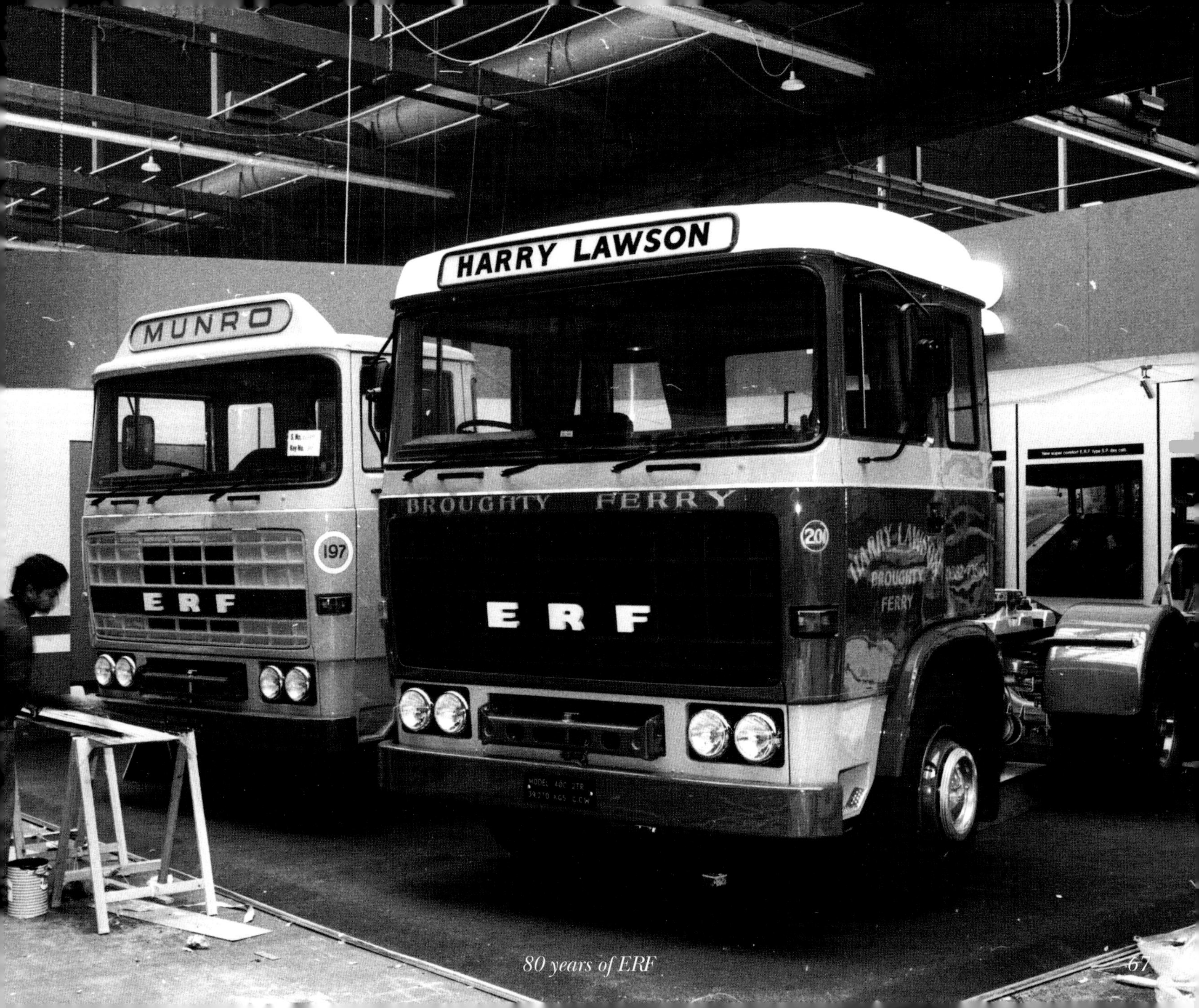
MUNRO
197
ERF
HARRY LAWSON
BROUGHTY FERRY
ERF

This early B Series unit, KTX 862P, is in the livery of Blue Line Transport of Tondy, Bridgend, seen with a neatly sheeted and roped load on a platform trailer. (PM Photography)

This Cummins-engined B Series, WGK 301R, in the fleet of Vine Products and Whiteways, is seen with a tank trailer in the 1980s, working between the company's wineries. (PM Photography)

A sleeper cab was produced by Jennings for the B Series. This had a flat-topped roof, as shown by rather weather-stained FRT 982T of F R Carter Ltd, of Thurston, near Bury St Edmunds, Suffolk. (PM Photography)

A works-built sleeper was also introduced in the late 1970s, as shown by TCR 952T, of Vectis Transport, based at Newport on the Isle of Wight, but which spent much of its time on the mainland. (PM Photography)

The B Series first appeared as an eight-wheeler, for operation at 30 tons gross, which proved popular with bulk tanker operators, like W O Sheeran of Middlewhich, whose Gardner-badged CRE 223T is seen here. (PM Photography)

The B Series eight-wheeler was also the basis of many tippers, like BKY 644T of Horrocksford of Clitheroe, which is fitted with an insulated body for aggregate or roadstone. (PM Photography)

This brand new-looking bulk tipper, VRY 928X, seen in the company of much older vehicles at a rally, was in the fleet of Murphy, based at Thurmaston, Leicester. (PM Photography)

Eight-wheeled platform vehicles were becoming quite rare by the time this Gardner 180-powered B Series was registered LBV 482T by Trinity Paper Mills at the end of the 1970s, but sometimes problems of access with artics still made the rigids more attractive to operators. (PM Photography)

For its animal feed deliveries, Dalgety chose the six-wheeled B Series chassis, operating at 24 tons gross, for this bulk-blower equipped tipper, VFN 893T. (PM Photography)

ERF introduced the M Series four-wheeled chassis for the 16 tons gross rigid market in the late 1970s, identified by the lower-mounted cab, with the headlights in the bumper. It was available with either a Gardner or Dorman V8 engine, as in BRY 614T of Federated Road Transport Services of Leicester. (PM Photography)

Some B Series were built as 'Chinese Sixes', although a few were rebuilt from older vehicles, fitted with the new cab. This is Gardner 180-powered CAD 468Y of well-known ERF operator Vic Haines of Pershore, which could have been either. (PM Photography)

Some B Series units were built with the eight cylinder Gardner 240, like day-cab-fitted CRN 842S, in the livery of Howarth Bros of Ingleton. (PM Photography)

Another B Series with the factory sleeper cab was DEK 855T in the Heatons fleet which was on contract to UK Corrugated. It was pulling a curtain-sided trailer, becoming more popular with many operators at the turn of the 1980s. (PM Photography)

These days, many tipper operators use articulated vehicles but, 30 years ago, this B Series eight-wheeled bulk tipper, CWR 264T, was typical of the Hansons of Wakefield fleet. (PM Photography)

The County of Stafford used this B Series eight-wheeler, TRE 148X, fitted with a hydraulic lorry loader to handle the test-weights, for its weighbridge testing unit. (PM Photography)

Unloading on a building site with its Hiab hydraulic lorry-loader, this B Series six-wheeler, OKX 535V, was part of the fleet of Anchor Roof Tiles of Leighton Buzzard. (PM Photography)

With a cattle box on its platform body, this Gardner 180-powered six-wheeler, NSF 322P, was in the fleet of R & D Runciman of Aberfeldy. (PM Photography)

Sporting a later-style Cummins badge, this B Series eight-wheeled tipper, UFR 940V, was fitted with a 'Task-Tip' aggregate body for its operator, Waddington Fell Quarries, of Clitheroe, Lancashire. (PM Photography)

80 years of ERF

The C Series featured an up-dated SP3 cab and various weight-saving features on the chassis. This Cummins-powered twin-steer C40 was displayed at the 1982 NEC Show in anticipation of the increase in permitted maximum gross vehicle weight, which finally materialised in 1983, increased from 32.5 metric tonnes to 38 tonnes. (CHC abg812)

Above: With 38 tonnes gross combination weight allowed on five axles, many operators opted for a two-axle unit and tri-axle trailer, like this C Series, DVW 474Y, of David Saunders of Pembroke. (PM Photography)

Right: Other operators, like Wyatt of Leeds, opted for a three-axle unit and tandem trailer, especially when the cost of new or up-grade trailers, such as tankers, were involved. Cummins 'Super E' Turbo-powered C Series, C535 VBF, proves the point. (PM Photography)

Axminster Carpets from Devon is another well-known name, with a fleet of long-lived ERF M16 rigids with personalised registrations, like 8 AXE from the mid-1980s and earlier OOO123W, both Gardner-powered. (PM Photography)

Eight-wheelers remained popular for certain work, like rubbish or scrap removal, as seen here with C Series, B 273 DMR, of Coopers Metals of Swindon. (PM Photography)

Over the years, many companies have been taken over or merged, or just worked together. This picture features three well-known names from the past, Haselden, Nuttall and A A Griggs, with this C Series 6x2 unit, C145 EBU, and tandem-axle curtain-sided trailer. (PM Photography)

This late Cummins Super 320-powered C Series, C526 UEH, was one of the well-respected fleet of Brian Harris, based at Widdecombe-on-the-Moor, Devon. (PM Photography)

80 years of ERF

This E16 6x2 twin-steer unit was in the fleet of R G Bassett of Tittensor in Staffordshire, which could be seen in most parts of the country for many years. (PM Photography)

Another well-known name from the past, G L Baker of London, on D 747 CLD, an early example of the next development from ERF, the E Series. (PM Photography)

The E Series was also available as an eight-wheeler. This bulk tipper, with Neville Charrold body, is in the striking livery of Longthorne & Sons of Hebden, near Skipton. (PM Photography)

Suttons of St Helens used this patriotic livery for many years on its fleet of British-built tractor units, like E412 VWM, a three-axle E Series, seen with a chemical tanker trailer and others from the fleet. (PM Photography)

For the maximum possible cubic capacity, draw-bar outfits have been popular over the years for light, bulky commodities like packaging. Here is an E Series rigid, K128 YDC, an E10-325 of Ranger Transport of Sedgefield, County Durham, in use for just that. (PM Photography)

Vic Haines' E12-270 curtain-sider, F312 UDG, has been fitted with a third axle with single tyres, to increase its maximum permissible gross weight and avoid axle overloads. (PM Photography)

80 years of ERF

Ansells Brewery wouldn't give a XXXX for anything but G769 WOY, a E8-265 and draw-bar trailer, fitted with sliding curtain bodywork, in the livery of the well-known Australian lager. (PM Photography)

Another three-axle E14 in a classic livery, E782 HRF, with a tandem-axle van trailer, was in the fleet of H Tideswell & Sons Ltd, of Kingsley, Stoke-on-Trent. (PM Photography)

Into the 1990s, with this E14 320 Cummins-powered two-axle tractor unit in the fleet of Nottinghamshire timber merchant John Brash. The company was know for its use of special narrow trailers with demountable frames for quick unloading of stacks of sawn timber. (Pm Photography)

An EC10 in the British Sugar fleet, M314 YEG, with a bulk tanker trailer. This was another company to favour the 'two plus three' configuration at 38 tonnes gross. (PM Photography)

ERFs have always been favoured by many of the major fuel companies, as exemplified by this EC10 three-axle unit, M944 MNB, in the Shell delivery fleet. (PM Photography)

This EC11 in the Castle Cement fleet, T296 RFL, was running on six axles, in anticipation of another uplift in the maximum gross vehicle weight, which is now 44 tonnes. (PM Photography)

During the 1990s, ERF's top-of-the-range EC tractor units, fitted with an extended sleeper cab, were known as 'Olympics', some of which remain in use with faithful operators. These were seen among the ERF display at Kelsall in 2012. (Author)

This funfair operator has upheld the tradition of using ERF vehicles previously in haulage fleets, rebuilt for their new purpose and finished in colourful liveries, as seen here on these E and EC Series, at the Bedford rally in 2012, although Cummins engines have replaced the legendary Gardner to power the lorries. (Author)

ERF continued to produce eight-wheelers in the 1990s, like this Skipton-based mixer-equipped EC11, with what looks like a personalised plate, J 16 RMX. (PM Photography)

The last 'real' ERF was the ECX, which appeared at the same time as the MAN take-over. This had the last version of the SP-type cab. In spite of the inroads from the continental manufacturers, ERFs continued to appear in many fleets, large and small, like this example, Y793 ODM, working for the Morrisons supermarket chain. (PM Photography)

After the MAN take-over, the first sign of its influence was seen with the ECS, which used a version of the MAN 2000 series cab, like this eight-wheeled tanker, Y861 KNB, of North-west based Carlton Fuels. (PM Photography)

The ECT was produced under the aegis of MAN. The early examples were mainly Cummins-powered, offering an alternative to the standard MAN fare. The cab, however thinly-disguised, still told you it was an ERF, like this artic tipper in the fleet of A J A Smith of Clitheroe, MX54 CEN. (PM Photography)

The ECT continued to appear in the major fleets. This one, DK04 RHJ, is a Wincanton vehicle, working on contract to clothing retailer, Matalan, which does not require the permitted maximum gross weight, so it is running on only four axles. (PM Photography)

The ECT remained in demand as an eight-wheeler. This one is the basis of a bulk-blower equipped tipper, YX08 EHW of grain and feed merchants, H Walton of Goole. By this time, the vehicle was most likely powered by an MAN engine. (PM Photography)

The very last ECT to roll off the production line in 2008 is used by enthusiastic owner, Barry Dancer, to move plant with a low-loader trailer. Registered OO08 ERF, it is seen here at a rally, with the REVS trailer and the first ERF. (PM Photography)